GETTING IN— THE RIGHT COLLEGE WITH THE RIGHT PLAN

GETTING IN— THE RIGHT
COLLEGE
WITH THE
RIGHT PLAN

IVY STYLE COLLEGE PREP SERIES

Edwina Armstrong, MA

CEO and Principal Educational Consultant at EAVisions and Former Director of Student Financial Services at Harvard University, Kennedy School of Government

*SpeakWrite Publications * Georgia*

Designed by Vince Pannullo
Interior Design, Charts & Tips: Edwina Armstrong
Illustrations on pages 60 & 95: Permission from iStockphoto.com
Illustration on page 29: Permission from UnSplash
Illustration on page 71: Permission from UnSplash (Steve Johnson)
Illustration on page 89: Permission from UnSplash (Kate Macate)
Other Illustrations: Personal Permission

Printed United States of America.
By One Communications LLC 800-621-2556

Library of Congress Cataloging-in-Publication Data
Name: Edwina Armstrong
Company: www.eavisions.com
Title: *Getting In—The Right College With The Right Plan:*
Answers and Tips All Students Need to Know
Series I: Ivy Style College Prep Series

ISBN: 978-0-578-64048-8 (Paperback)
First printing edition, 2020
SpeakWrite Publications
Hadley Township
Sugar Hill, GA 30518
Speakwritepub.com

CONTENTS

DEDICATION

To my parents, Frank and Georgia, you laid the right
foundation and sacrificed everything to give me the life you
only dreamt about. Your unconditional love and support
gave me thecourage to write this book.
Thank you for believing in me and loving me through my
season of transition. I love you, both.
Today is a New Day!

To my sisters and brothers,
Jacqueline, D'edra, Frank, Shirelle, Kimothy,
and Louise—
Thank you for participating in our Sunday and
Monday night calls, as we encouraged, prayed for, and
empowered one another by sharing our goals and
investment ideas. I love you all and appreciate the
gifts that you each carry.

To my nieces and nephews,
I love you all!
Brionna (Millionaire Mastermind), Corey (Chosen One),
Kashena, Natiera, Elijah, Kalifa, Bryan, Jiraye, Dominique,
Tati, Manyra, Mya, Kimyra, Abraham, Cyanni, Simone,
Kingsley, Kinsley, Josiah, Brooklyn, and Bentley

INTRODUCTION

Scenario 1 ~ Do you feel totally lost with the process of applying to college? In other words, you do not know where to look for the information, and you do not have anyone to turn to but the Internet?

Scenario 2 ~ Have your parents told you since the age of 10 that you were going to college, but now that you are older, you have no clue of how it is going to happen?

Scenario 3 ~ After applying for college, did you run to the mailbox every day looking for the decision letter from your preferred school, only to find an admission acceptance letter with no offer of financial aid?

Scenario 4 ~ Have you been sitting for hours trying to figure out what to include in your college essays that would make yours stand out?

If you can relate to any of these scenarios, then this book series is for you.

Getting In—The Right College With The Right Plan is the first in the Ivy Style College Prep educational book series that provides prospective college students with insight, tips, and tools they can use to address and tackle the most commonly asked questions junior and high school students ask regarding the college application process.

Below are seven of the most frequently asked questions by prospective college students:

- Where do I start?
- What should I pursue (Job vs. Career)?
- What should I consider when selecting schools?
- How do schools view my application(s)?
- What do I write about in the college essays?
- Who should I ask for a recommendation?
- How am I going to pay for college?

When I first started writing this book, I asked myself an extremely important question—What is the purpose for writing this book, when there are thousands of books, guides, and articles already in publication that explore and explain the college admissions process? Some of the information is just a click away (Internet) or a visit away (in local bookstores or in the office of high school guidance counselors). Additionally, more than ever before, there are hundreds of independent educational consultants attempting to share this information outside of the school setting, through one-on-one or group sessions, webinars, articles, and via media coverage. Yet, students and families still feel that the college admissions process is costly, overwhelming, and burdensome.

My Story

When I applied to college in the 80's and 90's (shh…stop trying to figure out my age), I did not have access to nearly as much information that is so readily available to students today. My guidance counselor provided very little "guidance" and insight on the admissions selection and application processes. With no guide or reference book, my counselor quickly directed me, and many of my classmates, to apply to a local community college. Now, while there is nothing wrong with community colleges, the choice to attend one is usually centered around a specific need, be it financial, academic (to test the academic waters), or personal (e.g., a student is not ready to move away from home to attend college out of state). None of these fit my personal circumstances. I was interested in attending a four-year college/university that was located out of state.

Being provided with such limited information and direction forced me to initiate the process on my own. One of the first things I did was to start completing college applications that were mailed to my home. I had never even heard of half of the colleges or universities. But I figured I'd play the numbers game and increase my odds. It wouldn't be too long before I stumbled across one of the most dreaded acronyms—FAFSA. *What in the world is this FAFSA?* You mean, I must ask my parents for their personal financial information to complete this form and send it to a place I never heard of before in my life? I then began to realize that applying for college without no real preparation wasn't going to be no easy task. My parents had every intention on me attending college after graduating high school; however, we did not have a concrete financial plan. When I was admitted to college, I, personally, had no financial means to pay for tuition. Therefore, my parents had to cover the tuition and room and board out-of-pocket, less the amount that I received from a federal student loan. I had no knowledge on outside scholarship opportunities or how to obtain one, which left the cost of college education on the shoulders of my parents.

Given the brief outline of my personal experience described above, please allow me to caution you to not make the same mistakes I made when it comes to applying for college, including the cost of repayment. It took me 17 years to completely payoff my undergraduate debt. My income fell short of my household expenses, so I applied for alternative repayment plans that did not work in my favor in the long run. Although my monthly payments were more manageable, I became comfortable with making the minimum payments, even after my income increased. I was repaying my student loans, all while I was paying monthly expenses that included a mortgage payment of approximately $1,200, a car payment of $300, condo association fees of $450, and other necessary costs. This does not have to be your story. There is too much information out there today, and you just need to know where to find it and how to obtain it.

Despite a broken college admissions process, millions of students (70% of high school seniors) navigate through the admissions application maze and enroll in college for the first time (United States Department of Labor, 2017). Unfortunately, more than 45% of these seniors do not enroll in their first-choice college or university due to financial reasons. It does not end there. Nearly 30% of high school seniors who do not enroll in college after high school graduation either have no interest, cannot afford it, or they do not want to undertake the daunting process. This should not be the case in 2020.

Lastly, I hope that this book will help the reader to *take immediate action* with simple homework assignments that are included at the end of the chapters, which will allow the reader to take control of the process with better clarity and ease.

Partnership

I am is partnering with you by sharing critical tools, tips, and advice to plan your college experience and before professional career. As your partner, my goal is to empower you to begin the college process with the right mindset, build your knowledge base with information on hundreds of career professions and salary ranges, help you select the right schools for your current and future interests, equip you with information on what schools to apply to, show you how to take your demographic profile and turn it into a solid essay, submit strong recommendations, and **show you the money**.

That is, provide you with information on how to find scholarships (merit and need), help you apply for student loans in a fiscally-responsible way (i.e., only borrowing what you 'need'), and help you position yourself to conquer the financial aid frenzy without feeling overwhelmed or frustrated.

Taking action is paramount to having success throughout the college enrollment and graduation processes. The ball is in your court!

CHAPTER 1

WHERE DO I START?

HABITS AND DISCIPLINES

QUOTE: *"The question I ask myself like almost every day is, 'Am I doing the most important thing I could be doing?' ... Unless I feel like I'm working on the most important problem that I can help with, then I'm not going to feel good about how I'm spending my time."* ~ *From* **Marcia Amidon Lusted's** *biography* <u>Mark Zuckerberg: Facebook Creator.</u>

APPLYING for admission to college is not the easiest process to navigate. Therefore, your approach is key to simplifying the process. Developing the right mindset and constructive habits are extremely important when starting the college process. Stephen Covey's book, *7 Habits of Highly Successful People*, which was the framework for Sean Covey's book, *7 Habits of Highly Successful Teens*, has identified several habits that highly successful people exercise regularly. In summary, a positive attitude and employing good habits attract positive or good situations and circumstances in our lives. Negative or bad habits attract negative or bad situations and circumstances. What are you attracting?

All students can learn from Stephen and Sean Covey's principles on adopting positive habits, which have a proven track record of success in the lives of teens and adults around the globe. Here are ways you, the student, can apply positive principles and habits to the college enrollment and application processes. The Habits include:

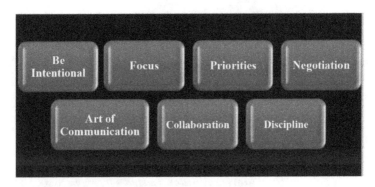

Developing healthy habits, whether young or old, can change your life and circumstances.

BE INTENTIONAL

Being Intentional is taking responsibility of a situation or circumstance and directly influencing it to yield a specific result or outcome. A person who is intentional takes the initiative to start the college process and does not wait for their parents or guidance counselor to do the work. The *'modus operandi'* or *'mo'* of a reactionary person, is to respond to a problem or circumstance from a short-sided view or based on their emotions. They tend to wait for things to happen to them by passing on the responsibility of applying to college to someone else. Reactive people make excuses and/or find something or someone else to blame for their behavior. "If the weather is good, they feel good. If it isn't, it affects their attitude and performance, and they blame the weather," says Covey. So, here you have it—intentional or reactive! Which one are you?

Being intentional is not just going to happen automatically; it's a habit that you MUST develop. This habit is not an overnight phenomenon or sensation. It takes deliberate practice. There are certain circumstances that can catch you totally off guard. However, your response to a situation is key. You cannot change external forces, but you can change or control how you respond to the circumstances.

I, too, had to develop constructive habits when I was in college, and most certainly, during my professional career. I turned to Dr. Caroline Leaf's book, *Who Switched Off My Brain?* Her book helped me to identify toxic thought/ thinking patterns that were influencing my decisions. Once I did, I had to develop concrete principles and action steps that would change my thoughts, behavior, and speaking patterns. I recommend her book to you. You may want to find your own resource guide to help you adopt healthy habits, and that is okay. But trust me when I say that it pays to have a healthy approach when going through the admissions process.

Tip 1   Take the initiative and start researching schools you would like to attend, and do not wait on your guidance counselor or your parent(s).

There are several ways to begin to collect information via the Internet or at your school or local library, because there are several criteria you will need to consider before selecting a college. You can start with a Google search of colleges in your local area. This will give you a list of schools you can research. If you already have a college or university in mind, then start there. Researching schools is step one. This step simply aids you in exploring and increasing your options. As a prospective college student, you are taking matters into your own hands and not waiting for someone to lead you in searching for the colleges or universities of your choice.

Tip 2   Identify schools that align with your unique goals and objectives and make a list of their criteria and requirements. Most schools will require all or most of the following:

- Common Application or Independent Application
- Essay(s)
- Transcripts
- Scores (ACT, SAT, PSAT)
- Extra-curricular activities
- Recommendations
- Application fee

You are now leading the charge. You now know which schools require the common application and which schools require an independent application process. You have an idea of the average GPA and test score requirements of the students attending respective schools. As a consultant, I am asked frequent questions about transcripts and standardized tests. Please keep in mind that the admissions process is more than just test scores and grades. Most schools take a holistic approach to the application/evaluation process. However, if your grades fall below the reported average, in the spirit of being proactive, you should begin to take measures to improve your grades. I will talk about this subject in greater detail later in the book.

Tip 3   Using an online calendar, cell phone, or manual calendar, make note of interested schools' deadline dates. After you record the deadline dates, schedule 30/60/90-day alerts. This will remind you that your application is due in 90 days, 60 days, and 30 days. This system will become very handy to multi-task completing essays, requesting transcripts and recommendations for schools in which you are applying.

As you continue to take the initiative in this process, being proactive will become a lifestyle and not just a word you use.

Focus

When you become focused, you place your concentrated attention on the main event until completion or you have reached a desired goal or destination. Stephen Covey suggests, "Begin with the end in mind." Essentially, you want to begin the admissions process with a clear vision of your desired outcome. Set attainable goals and clear objectives on meeting them. Stay focused and stretch your muscles of intent to make things happen.

Tip 1   Use your creative imagination. What is it that you envision taking place in your life in the next day, month, year, two years, or three years? What do you want to be? Who do you want to become?

Tip 2   Challenge yourself by setting realistic goals. A measurable goal can be to increase your high school GPA. To accomplish this goal, you must set clear objectives and strategies. One such objective could be to increase your study time by an additional 2 or 3 hours or consult a tutor for help. It might seem like an aggressive goal, but it is attainable if you want it bad enough.

Tip 3   Objectives without the right habits will not work. What habits and disciplines are you willing to exercise (or adopt) to make the 3.7 or the 4.0 GPA possible? If you are the type of student who procrastinates with your studies and waits until the last minute to complete your homework, what are you willing to change or do differently to become more proactive when it comes to studying and completing your homework? Remember, habits are choices you make or fail to make.

PRIORITIES

Priorities! What are your priorities? When I started listening to and reading personal development tapes and books, many of my mentors would say, "Keep the main thing, the main thing." This simply means that you focus on the important things and put aside the small things, the inconsequential things that have no significance. At the end of the day, what is more important to you, getting to the next mission on GTA-5 or obtaining a college education? What are your priorities?

> Tip 1   Perform a mental assessment. What do you focus your time on? Are you spending 2 to 3 hours playing on X-Box, and then you devote 30 minutes to researching colleges, drafting your essays for college, or studying for the SAT or ACT?

Identify things that stand in the way of you moving closer to your set goals and work on removing the distractions. Decide what is more important to you, downloading the newest App or obtaining a college education? Keep the main thing the main thing!!!

NEGOTIATION

Many young students do not have a clue when it comes to how to negotiate a win–win situation. Stephen Covey says, "We think about succeeding in terms of someone else failing—that is, if I win, you lose; or if you win, I lose. Life becomes a zero–sum game."

When it comes to the planning your secondary education, you need to adopt the attitude that you have something to bring to the college table or classroom. Your perspective, knowledge, gifts, and talents make you an asset to any college. Thus, enrolling in college creates a win–win situation. The college gains your skills, talents, and experiences, and, in turn, you are gaining knowledge and academic training to take your career to the next level. This will help with your college search. Select the schools that align with your values and interests. This is helping you create or negotiate a win–win situation. The institution has what you need and you, the student, have what they want.

Tip 1   Remove the competitive process and adopt a more value-based attitude. Identify your strengths, skills, talents, and experiences that give you a unique voice.

This process will become extremely beneficial when you begin drafting your essay. For your story is what makes you stand out from the crowd.

Art of Communication

The 'art' of communication is to listen more than to speak. This is a powerful skill that very few people master. We show that we value other people when take the time to "hear" what they are trying to communicate to us. Most people want to be heard by getting their point across, even if it means cutting someone off and interrupting the conversation to add their two cents. Stephen Covey asserts that, "By doing so, you may ignore the other person completely, pretend that you're listening, selectively hear only certain parts of the conversation, or attentively focus on only the words being said, but miss the meaning entirely."

During my tenure at Harvard Kennedy School, our recruiting efforts included discussing some of the many benefits of being at Harvard. One of the benefits was what we called the Sixth Class. The Sixth Class were study groups that allowed students to engage in dialogue and learn from one another. Another word for this is peer learning.

When you begin the college preparation stage, you should solicit the participation of your peers. You do this by simply engaging them. Everyone brings their own set of skills and experiences to the classroom. Their background, skills, and experiences often shape their perspective on circumstances, situations, and world events, just as yours do for you. Seek the feedback of others and respect their opinion. Your friends just might have different ideas and insight on selecting a college program that you may have never thought about before. For example, a female student from India may have a different perspective on domestic and international human rights than a student from New Hampshire. Thus, the key to communication is developing your listening skills and being intentional about the words you use.

Tip 1   Communication is essential to developing healthy relationships inside and outside the classroom. Do not underestimate the experience of your fellow classmates. This is a prime opportunity to learn and share ideas, tips, and insight on the college selection and application processes.

Tip 2   Practice holding your point until the other person shares their complete thought or idea. Listening to others can stretch you and provide greater insight on personal and professional matters.

COLLABORATION

Collaboration is about building a team of like-minded individuals for a common goal of finding a solution to a pressing problem. Stephen Covey calls this "synergy." Solving a problem takes a group effort to invent creative ideas and solutions. It takes a team aligned with a common mission or objective to come together. The same is true when it comes to business. It is common for businesses to align with organizations that have a common mission to solve world or global issues such as poverty, homelessness, and human trafficking. This same concept applies to you, the student. When you are researching colleges you might like to attend, you want to look for those programs that align with your values, skills, and talents. Students who have identified schools whose cultures align with their skills and talents are more likely to end up in a highly collaborative educational environment.

Tip 1   Be clear on your values, ideas, opinions, skills, talents, and experiences. During your college search, look for schools that align with your values and mission in life. For some, it may be important for you to align with a school that challenges the status quo or your ideas.

Tip 2   Developing a College Action Team with your peers can be a valuable commodity. Cherish the connection of others.

DISCIPLINE (BALANCE)

Constantly improve yourself, your skills, and talents through personal development, commitment, and discipline. Discipline starts by identifying the necessary steps it take to reach your end goal and making a commitment to follow those steps to completion. It is important to become a student who continually exercises the disciplines of being focused, intentional, establishing priorities, becoming a negotiator, improving communications skills, and engaging in collaborative efforts. By doing so as a daily practice, you are essentially refining and polishing your skills, talents, and abilities, which will inevitably allow the best version of who you are to emerge.

Tip 1   Commit to these habits and other positive habits before, during, and after the college process.

Tip 2   Make these habits a priority in your life. These habits have changed many students' lives, and it will do the same for you.

Tip 3   Embrace change, as it can be a gift.

JOURNAL EXERCISE

Date: _____

Identify 7 current habits:

_____

_____

List 3 negative habits:

_____

_____

What habits from this list do you currently exercise?

_____

_____

What habits from this list do you need to work on?

_____

_____

Are there other habits you could stand to adopt?

_____

_____

List 1 habit you can adopt today (diligence, ambition, optimism, excitement):

_____

_____

CHAPTER 2

IS COLLEGE FOR ME?

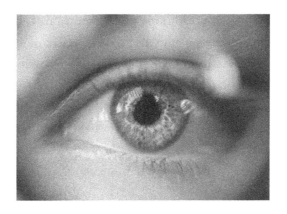

If money was no object, what could I
see myself doing?

QUOTE: *"Expect the unexpected. And whenever possible, be the unexpected."* ~ **Jack Dorsey**, *Twitter CEO*

THE increasing costs of college, the intimidating admissions processes, and extremely high loan debt raises the question from high school students, "Is college worth it?" I have been bombarded with the questions regarding the relevance of enrolling in college.

Traditionally, the college experience was supposed to give students an opportunity to stretch outside of their comfort zones, sharpen their skills and talents, challenge antiquated beliefs, and stimulate their intellectual curiosity. It was where students developed team-building skills and expanded their global perspective on crucial controversial issues, such as human rights, homelessness, poverty, economics, law, political injustice, ethics, and technology and transportation. Higher educational institutions were responsible for creating an environment where students from all walks of life could gather in the classroom setting to share diverse ideas, interests, and experiences. Then, at commencement, students were embarking on a new season of their lives by taking their learned wisdom, knowledge, professional, and personal skills into the marketplace to transform the world. Today, students are faced with the weight of the price tag of college tuition.

Listed below are statistics that high school students face:

- The average cost of tuition at a 4-yr. public college is $19,500 and $41,500 at a 4-year private college (U.S. Department of Education, National Center for Education Statistics, 2019)
- A third of students leave college for various reasons—financial reasons

- The average loan debt of a college graduate is approximately $30,000, and it is much higher for students attending a private college or Ivy League School
- Approximately 70% of graduates work in an industry different from the field they pursued in college.

With such bleak numbers, it is no wonder that students question whether they really need a college degree. Why incur the debt just to work at a job outside of their field of study? These are relevant questions and considerations.

The purpose of this chapter is not to answer the question of whether college for you, but it is to help you to become crystal clear on your personal intentions and how to get the best out of your college investment. Making the decision to go to college, despite the overwhelming process, and selecting a viable career track is an important decision to make early on in life, especially when you are making a heavy financial investment. The Association of American Colleges & Universities (AAC&U, Spring 2013) highlighted the survey results from the Cooperative Institutional Research Program at the University of California–Los Angeles, which found that approximately 86 percent of the freshman students indicated that the number one reason they were pursuing college degrees was, "to be able to get a *better* job" (Pryor et al. 2011, 9; emphasis mine). Statistically speaking, over the course of four years, a quarter of the students will drop out of college, for several reasons, including financial issues, family obligations, and academic issues. Of the total number of graduates, more than 60% will not find a job in their targeted profession.

In my 18 years of experience in Financial Aid at Harvard Kennedy School and my ten years as an independent consultant, these are some questions and factors I advise students to consider when going to or returning to college:

- What is your motive for going to college (family tradition or to get a good job)?
- What is your career interest and what could you see yourself doing if all your needs are met (motivator)?
- When should you undertake this venture (after completing high school or after getting a couple of years of work experience)?
- How are you going to make this happen (self-pay, grants, and/or loans)?

These questions were designed to give students a starting point of creating a strategic plan for successful college enrollment and completion. Now, it is time for you to evaluate yourself and what is best for you, personally.

Why are you going to college?

Traditional Students

- For traditional students (18-24), is it to make your parent(s) happy or proud of you? Depending on your background, this reason can either motivate you to succeed, or it can be the driving force of resentment.

Nontraditional Students

- For nontraditional students (independent students in transition, adults returning to school, military individuals), do you want to attend a 4-year college/university to get the skills needed for career advancement, or can you participate in a personal development program that will give you the practical skills needed for personal and professional success?

All Students

- Is it for a higher paying position? A college degree does not necessarily equate to a good job with higher pay and benefits.
- Is it to practice in a specific area of interest (i.e., law or medicine)?
- Is it to become an expert in a certain field such as psychology, social work, or PhD – level research, etc.?

Keep in mind, however, that a college degree does not necessarily equate to a good job with higher pay and benefits.

Who are you going to college for? Is it for yourself, your parents, or both?

Traditional Students

- Is it for the community or starting the family legacy? Keep in mind that the weight of being the first to attend college can be the motivator for huge success or discouragement, particularly when you don't get the grades you were expecting.

Nontraditional Students

- Is it to maintain or advance your position at work?

All Students

- Is it for personal or professional growth?
- Is it for the family to maintain the tradition of obtaining a college degree?

What is your career interest vs. hobby interest?

Traditional Students

- Is it to help people?
  This is a pretty general goal. Start focusing on how you would like to impact or influence the lives of others.

Nontraditional Students

- At life's crossroads, what could you see yourself passionately doing for the next 10 to 20 years?

- Are you the kind of person who needs to find your passion and then pursue it, or are you the kind of person who puts passion in everything you do? People bring passion and creativity to their work. If you are no longer feeling fulfilled with what you have been doing for the last 10/15/20 years, ask yourself what might be the cause. Were you looking for the work to bring passion and fulfillment to your life, or do you bring passion and fulfillment to the work? Are you growing as an individual?

All Students

- If money was not an issue, what could you envision yourself doing for 3/5/10/20/30/40 years?
- Do you need job security, or do you want to get paid from your production/results?
- Are you fascinated by working in Corporate America, in education, elected office, in government, at a nonprofit, or are you motivated by heading your own business?

When is the best time to attend college?

Traditional Students

- Will you attend straight out of high school or work for a few years before applying to college?
  Do your homework. Find out if the college you would like to attend prefers some work experience. Students who have work experience come to the

classroom with a theoretical and practical frame of reference.

Nontraditional Students

- Is now the best time to go back to school, considering all your personal obligations, such as family, job, and/or finances?
- *How* are you going to make attending college a reality, financially?

All Students

- Do you have scholarship support?
- Are you expected to contribute financially toward your college education?
- Do you or your parent(s) have the personal resources to cover the cost of college attendance?
- Do you have limited or no funds? If so, what financial strategy do you have in place to ensure successful enrollment and graduation?
- Have you completed the necessary research to locate outside scholarship support to help fund your education?

These are questions and factors you need to consider before going to school. There are no right or wrong reasons for considering attending college. However, you can make wise or rash decisions that can change the course of your life for many years. College is a serious commitment and financial investment. My hope in sharing this information is that you, as the student, know your "Why?" You must now hold yourself accountable, responsible, and committed to the decisions you make or have made.

After you answer all the questions, the next step is to decide which discipline or career path you want to study. In high schools across the United States, students are not informed about the plethora of career opportunities, particularly entrepreneurship. Therefore, they have limited knowledge and information about available paths. Consequently, they gravitate to what they see around them—the environment. For some, their family has already selected the career path that they are to take, while others have been given very little, if no guidance at all on a purposeful career path.

In my recruiting days at Harvard, I encountered hundreds of students who were undecided about the type of job or career path in which to pursue. This is not a bad thing. Most people go through this at several points in their lives. Even adults are known to have what's called a mid-life crisis. They hit a dead end and start thinking there must be more to life than their present reality.

The goal of this chapter is to help reduce the percentage of students whose first job is in a totally different field than their course of study. Think about it this way: You are repaying college loans for a degree that you are not using. First things, first. Ask yourself what could you see yourself doing, if money was no object (labor to obtain)? Are you looking for a job or a career? A job is temporary or short-term. Careers, however, include lifework planning—academic and professional training in a specific industry or multiple industries. At the back of the book in Exhibit A is a list of more than 100 professions and their respective salary ranges. The purpose of the list is two-fold—to provide you with career options and to help you narrow down your college selection.

Tip 1   Become crystal clear on your "Why"?

Tip 2   Evaluate your personal intentions on going to college. If not college, then what? Write down 3 alternatives to college that will give you the same or better results.

Tip 3   Select 5 to 10 career opportunities that interest you for short-term and long-term gains (see Exhibit A).

Tip 4   Do your research and find the schools offering programs that prepare you for the selected positions.

JOURNAL EXERCISE

If money was no object, what could you see yourself doing?

_____

_____

From the list in the back, what career paths interest you?

1. _____   6. _____

2. _____   7. _____

3. _____   8. _____

4. _____   9. _____

5. _____   10. _____

CHAPTER 3

WHAT SHOULD I CONSIDER WHEN SELECTING SCHOOLS?

THE POSSIBILITIES!

QUOTE: *"I find it's better to focus on what's in front of you and to keep putting one foot in front of the other."*
-- **Mary-Kate Olsen**, *actress and business woman*

THERE are five questions you must answer when selecting a college. You get to choose where you want to go!

1. What goals and interests are important to me?
2. What school(s) line up with my unique needs and wants?
3. What school/college offers the programs I want to major in?
4. What is the investment in terms of cost, time, and resources?
5. What environment do I believe I will thrive in?

These are extremely important questions you want to consider when selecting a college. Unfortunately, many students do not enroll in their #1 school of choice. Several factors may contribute to this outcome; and, one is for financial reasons. If there is no financial plan or you wait until your junior or senior year to research financial resources, you have just placed a limit on attending your college of choice and the school you will ultimately end up attending. This is a sad truth, but it's reality. You cannot attend college without money exchanging hands between you, the institution, or an external organization supplying an awarded scholarship. Remember, FREE comes with a price! There is a transaction that takes place—talent and money.

SOLUTION

Selecting a college will require you to do your homework! I like to use the analogy of purchasing a car or a home. When you are purchasing a car, you do not buy the car until you test drive it and get an inspection, for the precaution that you do not want to buy a lemon. The same principle applies when you or your parents begin the process of purchasing a home. You/they researched several areas and then narrowed down the search, based on budget criteria and certain qualifying interests, such as having a good school system. Thus, it is a good practice to apply the same principles and priorities when it comes to selecting the college of your choice.

What are your top 9 priorities and interests?

1. Major

- Your career interests will determine the major you select. Many students select majors in Political Science, Philosophy, Forensic Science, Economics, or Criminal Justice. Select the major that will bring the most reward to you over the short-and long-term. Remember, enrolling in college is and will be one of the most expensive investments you will make, besides the purchase of a home, in terms of time, commitment, and money.

- STEAM areas: Colleges and Universities are encouraging more youth to consider careers in science, technology, engineering art, and math. There are several nonprofit and for-profit organizations and businesses offering scholarship support to youth groups to pursue careers in the STEAM disciplines, starting with the federal government's Committee on STEM (CoStem: www.ed.gov/stem).

The organizations playing a role in the STEAM/
STEM Committee are focused on five key areas:

o   Improve STEAM/STEM curriculum in
    grade school
o   Increase youth commitment in STEAM/
    STEM school
o   Improve by sustaining STEAM/STEM expe-
    rience for undergraduate students
o   Increase the presence of those historically
    underrepresented groups
o   Create graduate opportunities for the future
    workforce

As you can see, there is a comprehensive effort
to increase youth involvement in STEAM/STEM
fields of study and careers. At the end of this book,
in Exhibit B, you will find a limited list of colleges
and organizations involved in the STEAM/STEM
challenge.

The math discipline should not be confused with
field of finance. Math courses entail algebra,
statistics, geometry, calculus, and trigonometry.
However, Finance 101 will teach you accounting,
budgeting, balance sheets, and income statements.
Both disciplines will serve as assets to the student.
Nevertheless, finance is not a required course. It is
beneficial to know and understand that geometry

does not expose you to the concepts of accounts payable and accounts receivable, nor will it teach you how to balance your finances or a company's finances. Many students graduating from high school or college possess poor working knowledge of budgeting and finances. Whether one's concentration is in the Arts or Business, everyone could stand to learn the art and skill of money management.

2. Community College, 2-yr. Program, 4-yr. College or University, Professional Development Programs

- The type of college you apply to will depend on your personal preference. Some students feel they need a bridge before attending college; therefore, they apply to a community college to get a taste of the 4-year college setting/environment. Other students enroll in a 2-year college program and walk away with an associate degree. More often, students enroll in professional development programs to enhance a specific skill or interest (i.e., technical field).

3. State School, Private, or Ivy-league

- Applying to and enrolling in an Ivy-league institution versus a state school is of personal and academic preference. There are multiple reasons why a student decides to apply to Stanford

University, Harvard University, Rutgers University,
or University of California @ Berkeley. Some of
those reasons range from program, major, academic
rigor, faculty expertise, geographical location,
student make-up, extracurricular involvement, career
opportunities, alumni network, or family influence.
You decide what is important!

4. Diversity

- Diversity and inclusion among the student body
  has become increasingly important to colleges and
  prospective students. Gender, political affiliation,
  religion, race, ethnicity, personal and work experience, socioeconomic status, physical disability,
  military service, and sexual orientation are all a part
  of the diversity agenda. Diversity is considered an
  asset on the college campus and the workforce. It
  will expand your knowledge base and promote a
  paradigm shift.
- The August 2009 issue of the U.S. News and World
  Report highlights eight reasons diversity matters on
  college campuses:

  - Expands worldliness (global perspective)
  - Enhances social development
  - Prepares students for future career success
  - Prepares students to work in a global society
  - Promotes creative thinking

- Increase your knowledge base
- Enhances self-awareness
- Enriches your perspective

As you can see, diversity enriches the college experience. If this information is not posted on the school's website, make a phone call and inquire about their commitment to diversity, if diversity is important to you.

5. Large or Small Classroom Size

- Some students perform at a higher level in a classroom with 10 to 30 students versus a class size of 70 or greater. These students prefer a more intimate setting with a low teacher-to-student ratio. Other students thrive in a larger setting or classroom environment. They are not intimidated by large groups. Know your comfort level in participating and engaging in classroom dialogue.

6. Faculty Expertise

- The desire to learn from expert faculty is just as important as selecting the right college or university. After you select a college and major, search the faculty profiles. Know which professors or lecturers specialize in your area of interest.

7. Financial Assistance

- Financial Aid plays a huge role in most students' decision to attend a specific college or university. There are various forms of aid, from university merit-based fellowships, need-based grants, state and federal programs (grants, work-study, and loans), and private loans. Apply for as much financial aid as available—institutional aid, state and federal aid, private grants (names and links at the end of book), and family financial support.

- Most schools, if not all, will post the total cost of attendance, which includes tuition, room & board, associated fees, and books and supplies. Pay close attention to the school's recorded total budget and average institutional scholarship or grant amount. The difference between the total budget or tuition and the scholarship amount is what you will need to cover with other forms of financial aid, such as federal and state grant and loan programs. This is an extremely important part of the decision-making process. However, this should not deter you from applying to any school. This information will give you the ammunition to take the necessary steps to secure various forms of aid to make the college of choice doable. This means, cover your bases and apply for all forms of financial aid and pay close attention to required deadline dates.

- Complete the Free Application for Federal Student
Aid (FAFSA) in January. Some students wait until
after they are admitted into a college before they
apply for financial aid. This is too late. Many schools
send the financial aid letter with the admission letter.
Therefore, it would behoove you to apply for aid
as early as possible (after January 1). Most schools
do not require an extra application for merit-based
fellowships. It is often based on factors such as
grades or the strength of your admission application
itself. I will cover financial aid in more detail later in
the book.

8. Career Services

- Job or career placement should be a matter of
interest/concern when selecting a college or university. What percentage of students find employment
upon graduation? This will give you an idea of
the resources available to you to secure a job after
earning your degree. Also, ask about available
internship opportunities. This will help you establish
a relationship with employers even before you graduate. You never know, your job just might be waiting
for you after graduation.

9. Alumni Services

- Alumni connection and involvement is a rich
resource available to students. The partnership

between the alumni network and the institution adds to the reputation of the university. Become knowledgeable of the existing alumni groups in your area as well as potential career opportunities.

Answering these 9 areas of interest will help you select the best schools that align with your personal goals and objectives.

Next Move:

Once you have narrowed down your college(s) of choice, attend an Open House or take an onsite or virtual tour. There are national and local college tours available for high school students. Taking a tour will expose you to the college or university's culture. You can sit in on live courses and hear students engage in dialogue on key issues and topics.

Live tours will give you the chance to meet faculty members (professors) and begin to establish a relationship with the school. You will also have the opportunity to meet current students and receive direct feedback on how the school and program are working for them. You can receive answers to your questions from the students.

- What is the campus culture?
- Are the courses rigorous and intellectually stimulating?
- What is the makeup of the student body?
- Are there available internship opportunities?

- What is the ratio of faculty to student?
- How is housing?
- What student organizations are they engaged in?

Ask students would they select the same school, if they had to start the school selection/application process over?

Do not let the opportunity to sit down and speak with representatives from admissions, financial aid, and career services pass you by. Let the school know you have a strong interest in attending, determine what financial assistance is available to make this all possible, and get an idea of the likelihood of finding a job once you complete your degree. Note that if the school has a separate application fee, this is a great time to talk to someone in admissions about a waiver.

If your finances are limited, taking online virtual tours are the next best thing. Many of the questions you have can be answered from the website. If you inform the schools that you are interested in attending and would like to speak with a current student, most colleges will put you in contact with current student ambassadors. You should ask the same questions listed above and more. It would also behoove you to talk to a representative from admissions, financial aid, and career services. Their input will be useful when you are making your final decision to attend or not attend.

Speaking with a representative from Career Services is not on many students' radar. However, students go to college to put themselves in a better position to receive a higher paying position. Therefore, it is crucial that you speak with this department via onsite or online tour. You want to know the percentage of students who land a job in the field of choice or interest after graduation. This is an important factor to consider, given the fact that you are about to invest two to four years at this institution, and you may very well have to repay student loans.

Preparing for school is an exciting, yet serious challenge. There are several organizations that can assist you with the vital information you need to make your college decision. Start with the College Board and stay away from businesses or organizations that offer to buy you a 'back door' admission seat, whether it is through athleticism or any other means. You have the knowledge and tools to get into the school of choice on your own merits.

Tip 1   Value others' ideas, opinions, and experiences; they are just as valid as your own.

Tip 2   Life is but a vapor. Cherish the connection of others.

JOURNAL EXERCISE

List the Top 20 Colleges you would like to attend. Remember, consider the career fields you already compiled in the previous chapter's exercise.

_____   _____

_____   _____

_____   _____

_____   _____

_____   _____

_____   _____

_____   _____

_____   _____

_____   _____

_____   _____

In order of priority, what is the top 7 colleges?

College 1: _____

College 2: _____

College 3: _____

College 4: _____

College 5: _____

College 6: _____

College 7: _____

For each college, complete the following:

Concentration of Interest:

Type of Institution (2/4 yr. or professional school; state, private, or ivy league):

School's reputation or ranking:

Classroom size:

Financial Assistance:

Faculty Expertise:

Student Diversity:

Career Services (job opportunities):

Alumni Resources

Important Note: Make sure you complete this exercise for each college listed above. This exercise will help you to narrow down your college selection. If you are interested in Science, Technology, Engineering, and Math, see Exhibit B for helpful resources.

CHAPTER 4

WHAT DO I LOOK LIKE ON PAPER?

YOUR "BRAND" = LEVERAGE

QUOTE: *"Do not be embarrassed by your failures, learn from them and start again."~* **Richard Branson**, *Founder of Virgin Group*

AFTER you select your top colleges, it is time to review the college application and admissions requirements. This chapter is all about LEVERAGING your brand by building and enhancing your skills and talents to stand out from the crowd and submit a competitive admissions application. The best time to begin to build your brand is in junior high school/middle school. Students and families, however, often wait until the junior or senior year in high school to begin the process or plan for college. This gives you very little time to build your brand and develop ways to best leverage your skills and talents.

You do not have to pay anyone to write your resume or essays, or take your SAT. If you start early in the process, while in junior high/middle school, or freshman year (9th grade), it will give you ample time to boost your academic scores, get involved in an athletic sport of interest or a student club, consistently participate in extracurricular activities at school or in your community, and research and apply to competitions, contests, summer institutes, and camps. The following is a list of leveraging points you can use to sharpen your skills and talents which will aid you in submitting a competitive application:

Leverage Points
Grades
Standardized Tests
Leadership
Extracurricular Activities
Entrepreneurship

Grades

Grades are one element colleges factor in as part of the admissions decision. Admissions representatives have stated that grades are an important part of your college application, particularly grades made during the 10th grade and 11th grades. Please pay close attention when you are applying for Early College Admission in the fall of your senior year (12th grade). You will be required to submit a copy of your transcript, and since you will have just started the first semester of your senior year, your transcript will only have the classes and grades that you have already completed. Thus, the Admissions representatives will be reviewing your classes and grades of your previous years in high school (9th–11th grades), particularly the most recent year you just completed, which is your junior year or 11th grade.

It is believed that the higher the grades, the more academically competitive you appear. However, with the applicant pools becoming extremely competitive, it will take much more than a 4.0 to stand out. To advance academic goals and competitiveness, students often take Advanced Placement (AP) or International Baccalaureate (IB) courses to get college credits as a way to demonstrate to the admissions panel that they can successfully handle college courses. Make sure the college you are interested in attending not only encourages precollege courses but accepts them as well. If you are interested in Advanced Courses, see your guidance counselor, visit Coursera.com, or follow the information on the College Board website for specific AP courses.

Important Note: Most admissions offices take a holistic approach by weighing several factors, not just grades. However, to remain as competitive as possible, it is important to use the other leverage points to add value to your application, particularly your essays and resume.

Standardized Tests (SAT, ACT, GRE, GMAT, LSAT, MCAT)

One of the top issues of concern for students of all backgrounds is standardized tests. Although standardized tests have a reputation for being culturally insensitive, colleges and universities still require these tests. However, there is a new wave of educational institutions that are moving away from requiring standardize tests as part of the admissions process. Make sure you check the college's website or contact the school directly to learn their exact requirements.

My advice to students is to take the tests several times, if you can afford to do so. This will give you the opportunity to identify your strengths and weaknesses and work on these areas. There are plenty of online pretests you can take to measure your progress. Keep in mind, schools take the highest score. If you work better with a group, I would recommend enrolling in a program like Kaplan or Princeton Review. You can take these tests while in junior high/middle school or after you begin high school. Taking the test early is for your benefit.

Do not become someone's statistic! "I'm not a good test taker." Do not become comfortable with repeating this statement. You are adopting someone else's opinion of you. This could very well be the case; however, most students who retake the standardized tests score higher/better. Therefore, you owe it to yourself to present the best application possible. Enroll in a tutorial or a summer program to learn the concepts and precepts in areas where you received low scores. When you take the pretests early in junior high/ middle school or high school, you have ample time to work on areas of weakness and turn these scores around.

Programs that help you prepare for standardized tests (e.g., Kaplan, Princeton Review) equip you with practical skills and techniques you can use and apply when taking these tests to enhance your score. There are several online programs that share tips and teach you techniques and strategies that you can use to minimize anxiety and help you apply the process of elimination methodology to choose correct answers. Talk to your guidance counselor today.

Leadership

Leaders are problem solvers, idea generators, innovative or inventive, resourceful, have a positive attitude as outlined in Chapter 1, and are action oriented. Building your leadership ability is a critical leverage point. You can develop leadership skills through an internship, employment, or volunteer activity. Work can give you valuable business insight and add practical skills to your theoretical knowledge base. What are you good at? What interests you? Follow this pattern and talk to your guidance counselor or your peer team.

There are other ways to develop leadership skills. I learned from John Maxwell that leadership encompasses influence and serving others well. Look for ways to serve others. Is there a class that you do very well in that someone else may struggle in? Serve them by becoming a tutor! What about student organizations and clubs? Serve your school and fellow classmates. You can start by volunteering to serve or participate in the Student Government organization at your school. The following year, you can step it up a notch by serving in a position. These strategies are targeted to helping you develop your leadership muscle. Some of you have already discovered the value of serving at your school and want to take your skills to a local level. In this case, you might want to look for organizations in your community that align with your goals and values. The Journal Exercise at the end of the chapter prompt you to list ways that you can stand out from the college applicant crowd.

Extracurricular Activities

Extracurricular activities help you build your resume and essays. Pre-college programs, academic and/or debate teams,

Creative Arts (music, dance, writing-literary), academic tutors or student advisors, activities and positions with student groups, true athletic programs, local and national competitions, and contests can help boost your leadership skills and add to your competitive edge. Quality over quantity is key. The following is a list of programs and camps that would be worth your while to research and submit an application.

Blue Print Summer Program	Boston Leadership Institute
Boston University Summer Journalism	California State Summer School (COSMOS)
Carnegie Mellon Summer Academy (SAMS)	Carnegie Mellon Summer Program for Diversity
Clean Tech	Cornell Humanities & Sunshine
Creative Communication Poetry Contest	DECA
Doodle for Google	Duke Tip Academy
Emory Pre-College	Federal Reserve High School and College Fed Challenge
First Lego League	Girls Who Code Summer Immersion Program
Google Science Fair	Harvard Pre-College Program
High School Debate Teams	ID Tech Camp & Programs
Mathcamp	Mathcounts (Middle School)
MIT INSPIRE	National Economics Challenge by Council for Economic Education
National Scholastics Press Association	National Youth Science Camp (NYSC)
New York Film Academy's Summer Film & Acting	NYU PreCollege Program
Public Policy and International Affairs Program	Science Olympiad
Stanford Summer Session	STEM Video Game Challenge
Technology Student Association	Thomas R. Pickering Foreign Affairs Program

Tufts Summer Study	Tulane University Emerging Scholars Environmental Health Science & Research Academy
UCONN Summer Program for High School	United States Academic Decathalon (USAD)
University of Chicago Young Scholars Summer Program (YSP)	University of Dallas Summer Program
University of New Hampshire Upward Bound Summer Program	University of PENN Program High School
Verizon App Challenge	Young Entrepreneurs Business Week (YEBW)

Free Programs, Associations, and Camps

Business Opportunity Summer Session	Carnegie Mellon University
Dartmouth Bound Summer Program	Peer Forward
Princeton Summer Journalism	Sadie Nash Summer Institute
Students of Color Alliance	The Philadelphia Magazine/PABJ Summer Editorial Fellowship (with Black Journalists)
Women's Tech Summer Program (with Massachusetts Institute)	YouThink College Camps

This is, by no means, a comprehensive list of awesome summer institutes, camps, national contests, competitions, and STEM/STEAM programs. However, this list should get you started. Fastweb has a list of more programs, if you are interested.

Another discipline that some students explore is entrepreneurship. Being an entrepreneur is not for everyone. However, if you do have that entrepreneurship bug, whether it is opening your own lemonade stand, fixing computers, building websites, freelance writing, starting an ecommerce store, or designing your own T-shirts line, the leadership skills you gain from your business are worth highlighting on your resume and in your essays.

Entrepreneurship

The process of becoming a business owner is a mystery to the average student. Most primary schools do not offer courses on entrepreneurship. The average student's first exposure to business ownership is from television, social media, or in the home. Investopedia highlights youth who are blazing the trail of entrepreneurship. For example, 14-year old Hart Main is the owner of male/masculine-scented candles. His initial investment was $100. Now, his candles are sold in more than 60 stores nationwide. Charlotte Fortin created a fashion line called Wound Up while she was in high school. Nine-year old Caine Monroy is the owner of an arcade and designs his own T-shirt line. His YouTube video has gone viral.

Another program gaining global exposure and attention is the Thiel Fellowship program. The co-founder of PayPal, Peter Thiel, created the program to provide the start-up capital for selected young entrepreneurs. Thiel Fellows must leave college to begin the fellowship. To date, the Thiel Foundation has funded over 60 business ventures. Fellows receive $100,000 to use at their discretion. The foundation is equipped to provide the necessities the new business owner needs to successfully launch their business, including a marketing team and venture capitalists. The point being made here is that these fellows are successful business owners that do not have a college degree. However, they do have the people and financial resources necessary to start and maintain a successful business, unlike the average business owner who does not have these things at their disposal. Additionally, these fellows have demonstrated a positive mindset by their habits, as described in the beginning of this book.

Let's look at the top global entrepreneurs—the billionaires. Do they have a college degree or multiple degrees?

Name	Business	Worth	College Degree(s)	Inherited or Self-made
Jeff Bezos	Amazon	$112B	Princeton University	Self-made
Bill Gates	Microsoft	$90B	Harvard University Dropped out	Self-made
Warren Buffett	Berkshire Hathaway	$84B	Columbia University (Master Degree)	Self-made
Bernard Arnault & Family	LVMH *Louis Vuitton Moet Hennessy*	$72B	Ecole Polytechnique de Paris	Inherited
Mark Zuckerberg	Facebook	$71B	Harvard University Dropped out	Self-made
Amancio Ortega	Zara	$70B	Dropped out of school at the age of 14	Self-made
Carlos Slim Helu & Family	Telecom	$67.1B	National Autonomous University de Mexico	Self-made

Charles Koch	Koch Industries	$60B	Massachusetts Institute of Technology	Inherited
David Koch	Koch Industries	$60B	Massachusetts Institute of Technology	Inherited
Larry Ellison	Oracle	$58.5B	Universities of Chicago & Illinois	Self-made

*Forbes 2018 list of top 10 Billionaires' Net Worth (3/6/18)

Approximately one third of the top ten billionaires dropped out of college or did not attend college. I am not condoning not going to college; however, I do want you to be very clear and specific on your career path and what is required to achieve success in that specific line of work. In a nutshell, if you do not embody the positive habits of successful teens, then entrepreneurship is probably not the profession for you. Get the degree!

Tip 1   Look for ways to leverage, build, and enhance your application.

Tip 2   Extracurricular activities are not an option but a "must."

Tip 3   The list of extracurricular activities is not to replace your current hobbies or interests but can be used to add to your experience in sports, music, student, or local government, etc.

JOURNAL EXERCISE

GPA: _____

How can you improve your GPA?

_____

_____

_____

PSAT Score: _____

SAT Score: _____

How can you improve your scores?

_____

_____

_____

What are your current hobbies, interests, and/or extracurricular activities?

_____

_____

_____

How can you build and enhance your extracurricular activities?

_____

_____

_____

_____

What are your current leadership skills and talents?

_____

_____

_____

How can you build and enhance your leadership skills?

_____

_____

_____

_____

_____

_____

_____

_____

_____

CHAPTER 5

HOW DO I START THE ESSAYS?

YOUR "STORY"

QUOTE: *"You never lose a dream. It just incubates as a hobby."*
~ **Larry Page**, *Founder of Google*

HOW do you look on paper? Not all colleges and universities require an interview as an admissions requirement. Therefore, it is critical for you to show admissions representatives who you are on paper. Completing your admission application is not a task you should enter lightly. Always keep in mind that you are one of many trying to secure a seat at the university you want to attend. I'm not saying this to discourage or scare you but to prepare you. What are your unique assets? What is different about you? What moves you? What makes you tick? What issues challenge you and ignite passion within you? Your story is your brand. No one can tell it better than you can.

When you start writing, think about what you want people to know about your personality and character. You do not have to be an orator or novelist to write with finesse. Essays that are unique stand out above the rest. The art of writing college essays is taking the opportunity to introduce yourself by showcasing your passionate ideas, your personality, your unique set of skills and talents, identifying the problems you would like to solve, and clearly communicating specific out-of-the-box experiences that have shaped your views and perspectives. You should also point out what you expect to receive and learn from the program, such as robust academic training. You want to be challenged academically and intellectually, and you are looking for an environment where you can confront old beliefs, have direct exposure to faculty research, peer learning, and a host of other skills.

College essays are affording you a special invitation to share with the Admissions Administration the thing that makes you like no one else—your brand. Do not be embarrassed or avoid writing about adversity, obstacles, and challenging experiences or circumstances. In them, contain lessons, keys, and nuggets for you to learn from, elevate your thinking, and move forward. Write about a tough position you found yourself in and what steps you took to turn the situation around. What did you learn from this situation? What would you do differently? It shows your resilience. This is not the time to talk about how academically smart you are. Your transcript will do that job for you. Simply put, show the administration who you truly are and what you are made of.

You have probably heard the saying that first impressions are lasting impressions. That holds true even when writing your college essays. The first couple of paragraphs will make or break you. This is not the time to second guess yourself or your abilities. How you see yourself, determines how others see you. If you have low self-esteem, unfortunately, that is what you project to others. Your level of confidence or lack thereof, is bound to come across. It is your responsibility to creatively pique the interest of the Admissions Administrator and give him or her a compelling reason to read your essays and offer you a seat in the newly admitted class. You chief goal is to make it difficult for the admissions representative to put your application aside.

My Story

I was on the road recruiting students for Harvard Kennedy School. I spoke to more than 100 students at this event (Urban League or Black Public Administrators/ professionals and they opened the doors to students). Many students who were confident in their academic abilities approached my table asking me what HKS could do for them. Some approached my table in an arrogant way. I overlooked their behavior and addressed what I believed was their central question(s). One African-American male student kept pacing back and forth near my table. I knew he wanted to stop and talk to me, but he was hesitant to do so. As some students have shared, the Harvard name itself can be somewhat intimidating. Nevertheless, some time later, this young man finally mustered the confidence and approached my table. What struck me was what came out of his mouth. He said, "I could never get into a school like Harvard. My grades are not good, and I'm not a good student." Usually, I dismiss comments of this sort and simply engage in small talk. But this particular time, I did something different. I told the young man to never let those words come out of his mouth again, because no one knows your history. When you are meeting a representative of a school that you are considering applying to, you have to remember that the school's representatives have no idea what your grades are like. As I shared with this young man, you need to develop the mindset and act as if you belong at the school.

The young man left and returned to my table. This time, with his parents. They thanked me for sharing words of wisdom. I'm not sure if my feedback had a profound impact in the young man's life, but I am pretty certain that he will of remember the words I spoke into his life.

If I can help anyone, let me start by saying that it is crucial that you not allow outside forces to affect your inner confidence and determination. It is easier said than done. We all have strengths and weaknesses. Do not focus on weaknesses, unless you are challenging yourself to turn your weaknesses, like bad test scores, into areas of strength. For example, if you know you are a bad test taker, schedule the standardize test early enough to retake, if need be. Another piece of advice is that, if you have not tested well, but you have high grades in certain subjects, then, when drafting your essays, highlight the courses in which you received good grades, and describe the steps you took to challenge yourself in your areas of weakness. Most, if not all, admissions offices take a holistic approach to the admissions process. This means, the committee weighs all areas. There is always balance.

"A person's strength is to know their weaknesses."
— **Russell Simmons**

Do not allow anyone to pigeon hole you or reduce you to a statistic. You are much greater than that.

ESSAY TIPS

"One important key to success is self-confidence. An important key to self-confidence is preparation."

~ *Tennis Great,* **Arthur Ashe**

While there is a plethora of tips and strategies on the art of writing essays, here are seven (7) fundamental tips to help you become confident with the college essay writing process. The tips mirror the successful habits described in the beginning of the book.

Tip 1   **Be Intentional** about creating a basic profile of yourself. This stage is called brainstorming. Start with ideas and thoughts about your personality traits; habits; challenges; dreams; goals; personal, professional, political, and social interests; and accomplishments etcetera, etcetera. Have fun with this exercise and take your time. If you become stressed out, step away and come back to the essay(s) later.

Tip 2   Review each essay and make sure you
         understand the questions and **underlining
         principles.** Learn to read between the lines.
         The reader is trying to gauge your character
         traits, passion, resilience, assets you bring
         to the school and, with some training, what
         your potential impact or influence on a
         national and/or global level will be.

Tip 3   **Be specific and stay focused.** At the end
         of the day, what is it you would like the
         reader to know about you? Begin to organize
         your profile points into short stories that
         would best answer the pertinent questions.
         Be descriptive in your essays and eliminate
         all fluff and babble. Demonstrate your
         creative reasoning skills.

Tip 4   As you share your vision, you must **be
         willing to be authentic and honest** with
         yourself and the Admissions Office. Share
         your qualities, habits, and experiences with
         the school representative and the lessons
         you learned from them. Keep in mind, you
         have the advantage by sharing your unique
         strengths that you bring to the classroom.
         Remember, the school is gaining your skills,
         talents, and experiences and, in turn, you are

gaining knowledge and academic training to take your career to the next level.

Tip 5   **Be creative and take strategic risks!**
As you begin to share your authentic self with the reader, be willing to talk about your strengths, weaknesses, failures, and successes. Remember this, challenges and failures are great teachers. What are some obstacles you have overcome? What did you do when faced with a daunting problem, and how did you go about solving the crisis or dilemma? What areas can you stand to improve in, and how can the school, program, professor expertise, or peer group relations help you gain the insight, knowledge, and enhanced skillset to take your career to the next level?

Tip 6   **Keep the main thing, the main thing.**
Make sure you stay focused on answering the questions based on your own experience. You do yourself a disservice by answering the questions based on what you think the committee wants to hear or what you think sounds good; yet, it does not reflect your true voice or experience. You may find that it is helpful is to center your attention on one essay at a time.

Tip 7   **Write, rewrite, and proofread your work.**
Put your new synergistic nature to work. If
you are like most students, you will write and
rewrite your essays several times; thereby,
polishing your work and removing gram-
matical errors. You may find it extremely
helpful to get a second pair of eyes to read
your essays. They just might catch something
that you may have overlooked. So value their
feedback!

Now you are ready to submit your essays. I cannot guar-
antee your admission to the college of your choice. However,
if you follow the tips and advice, you can be confident that
you gave this process your best.

The profile below is the demographic highlights of a
fictious high school student.

NAME: Diane Joseph
High School: Woodward
City, State: Edison, NJ

Personality:
Optimistic, Consistent, Risk-taker, Direct

Areas of Interest:
Law, Criminal Justice, Psychology

Challenges:
academically challenged in Math, but determined;

Professional Experience:
Summer work as Assistant to the Vice President of McDonald's

Extra-Curricular Activities:
Played Soccer for 3 yrs.

Athletic Involvement:
Played soccer for 3 yrs.

Clubs & Affiliations:
Student Government

Professional Experience:

Entrepreneurship Experience:

Career Goal(s):
Lawyer; study political science or criminal justice

Mentors/Coaches: Principal Dawson

Volunteer Experience: homeless shelter

GPA: 3.5 (strong areas:
English and Science)

3 Qualities:
Resilient, Decisive, Optimistic

Favorite movie:
Facing The Giants, Alex & Stephen Kendrick

Favorite book:
My Sister's Keeper, Jodi Picoult

Mock Essay

One of my favorite movies is "Facing the Giants." The main theme of the movie shows how one can face their fears through overwhelming adversity. In the movie, a football team had to face its fears, while demonstrating perseverance, tenacity, and determination. To overcome adversity, the coach and players had to face attacks and criticism in the community as well as their six-season losing streak. To do this, they had to change their preexisting beliefs about themselves and their team. This movie motivated me to apply to Rutgers University.

A native of Edison, New Jersey, I always wanted to be a lawyer. When I was younger, I found myself pretending to be in a court room on the playground, as I defended my classmates or friends who were falsely accused or who ended up in some type of fictitious legal trouble. I knew it was going to take more than my innate ability to defend the underdog to be a successful lawyer. Getting good grades and being involved in school and the community were critical to being accepted by competitive colleges and universities.

As a sophomore, my grades were strong in math and science courses; however, I was challenged in sociology and history. To turn this situation around, I had to do the very thing the team in "Facing the Giants" did; I had to face my own giants. My usual study pattern was studying for an hour for each of my courses. But I discovered that I needed to consistently study additional hours in subjects that challenged me. This meant, I studied two to three hours in sociology and history. It paid off! I saw my grades improve—a C went to a B and then to an A. I followed this study habit/regimen for the remainder of my high school years.

There is a parallel between what I did and what the football team did in "Facing the Giants. The Shiloh Eagles (the name of the football team) did not just fold their hands and resume business or practice as usual. They changed their normal practice routine. The coach challenged the team's leader to do the death crawl blindfolded with another team member strapped to his back. I learned if I wanted something I've never had, I had to do something I've never done. This same attitude attracted me to Rutgers University. Your reputation for being a university that is a forerunner for change you want to see by leading from the front lines and not the sidelines. Courses such as Business, Torts and Intellectual Property, Constitutional Rights Clinic, and Advanced Metropolitan Equity will challenge my intellectual curiosity, while allowing me to gain the knowledge and skills needed to change policy and enforce the liberties of the citizens of New Jersey by promoting fair housing, education equality, and health parity.

Rutgers has maintained a renowned reputation for teaching and training students who are out of the box thinkers. Studying under such scholars as Matthew Bell, Professor of Law and Diane Dabush, Assistant Professor of Law, will allow me to challenge the status quo. I want to be immersed in an educational culture where the student body, representing 80 different nations, is comprised of ardent thought leaders who can come to the table to engage in open dialogue on conflict law and national security, yet eager to challenge their long-held beliefs on human rights and social justice. For these reasons, Rutgers University stands among the best. I want to be a part of the distinguished alumni network. It is my hope that the Admissions Office grants me a seat at the table.

Journal Exercise

Date: _____

Personality:

_____

_____

_____

_____

Challenges:

_____

_____

_____

_____

Professional Experience:

_____

_____

_____

Extra-curricular Activities:

_____

_____

_____

_____

Clubs & Affiliations:

_____

_____

_____

_____

Career Goal(s):

_____

_____

_____

_____

Hobbies:

_____

_____

_____

_____

Volunteer Experience:

_____

_____

_____

_____

Mentors/Coaches:

_____

_____

_____

_____

Three Qualities:

_____

_____

_____

_____

Name 2 Favorite Books:

_____

_____

_____

_____

GPA: _____

SAT Score: _____

ACT Score: _____

Draft Essay:

_____

_____

_____

_____

_____

_____

_____

_____

_____

_____

_____

CHAPTER 6

WHO SHOULD I ASK FOR A RECOMMENDATION?

STRONG RECOMMENDERS

QUOTE: *"Never give up. Today is hard, tomorrow will be worse, but the day after tomorrow will be sunshine."* ~ **Jack Ma**, *CEO Alibaba*

SELECTING the right recommender is equally important to the entire application process. I recall reading an application in which the student had a strong GPA, high GRE scores, and excellent essays. However, the student had weak recommendations. Students often put most of their time and effort into other parts of the application and neglect a critical part of the process, which is requesting recommendations from the right people. Do not become so desperate with the recommendation process that you ask just anyone to provide a recommendation on your behalf. It becomes obvious to an admissions representative that you put no or very little thought into who you selected to provide a recommendation. You should always get a recommendation from someone who knows you and can attest to your academic or professional skills, talents, and strengths. Do not overstep this important step. Keep in mind, recommendations are just as important as the rest of your application.

From a reader's perspective, it is quite simple to determine if the recommender knows the applicant by the choice of words written in the actual recommendation letter. I will let you in on a secret. A statement that is common in recommendations from a teacher/professor, lecturer, or counselor is to provide a ranking of the applicant's academic performance and strength in reference to the entire class or pool of students that they have taught or mentored. This means, if a teacher has taught 200 students, they will let the reader know how you rank in comparison of the entire class. For example, the teacher may express this fact by simply stating: "Out of the 200 students that I have taught during my 5-year tenure, Lisa/Jonathan, ranks in the top 5%." This is a impactful statement for a reader to consider. This means, you are ranked in the top 10 out of 200 students. Another powerful impact that a recommendation can have is when the recommender uses certain statements or words. Here are two examples:

- Robin/Robert is the most exceptional student that I have taught a X University.
- Robin/Robert is one of the most exceptional students that I have ever taught in my 20-year tenure at X University.

Now, hopefully this type of statement is not coming from your gym teacher because it will not have the same impact or carry the same weight as it would coming from a science, language arts, history, or math teacher. The same holds true if you are a college student applying for a seat in a graduate program. It is important when your teacher can speak well of you by highlighting how well you grasp concepts and precepts of the lessons, if you demonstrate intellectual curiosity (out of the box thinker), take the lead in groups, and execute assignments and projects well. It speaks volumes when a teacher/professor is impressed with a student's talents, qualities, skills, abilities, positive habits, and balanced emotions. A good recommendation contains "specific" language and gives specific examples of a student's strengths and abilities.

I do not mean to belabor this point. However, I would urge you to build a credible relationship with your instructors. Be careful of submitting standard recommendations.

Guidance Counselors and teachers can become inundated with drafting recommendations for college bound students. Therefore, you should request a recommendation early as possible.

Tip 1   Build credible relationships with your teachers, instructors, mentors, coaches, and supervisors.

Tip 2   Strategically select academic and/or professional recommenders who will speak highly of you.

JOURNAL EXERCISE

Date _____

List the names of potential Academic Recommenders:

_____

_____

_____

_____

_____

List the names of potential Professional Recommenders:

_____

_____

_____

_____

_____

CHAPTER 7

HOW AM I GOING TO PAY FOR COLLEGE?

FINANCIAL AID

QUOTE: *"Life is not measured by the breaths you take, but rather by the moments in life that takes your breath away."*
~ **Unknown**

PLANNING and investing in your college education are just as important and crucial as purchasing a home.

Most people will not purchase a home without adequate planning. When a family or individual considers buying a home, there is significant planning that takes place. Very few individuals have a funds equal to the amount of a down payment sitting in their bank account waiting for a rainy day. Well, the same thought and planning needs to take place when a family considers a child's college education. This, too, takes some planning, particularly financial planning.

Educational and financial strategies are crucial to successfully enrolling and graduating from college. There is a strong probability that a down payment, or deposit, is needed to get into college. This concept is called "Student or Family Contribution." This means that you or your parent(s) may be required to contribute toward your education. In other words, a personal monetary investment is required. If tuition costs $24,000 and the school provides financial support in the amount of $12,000, you and/or your parents will need to cover the $12,000 balance. Now, the question that remains is, how will you pay the balance? Do you have the personal financial resources, or will you need to borrow funds to cover the balance? If you need to borrow, how is your credit? Is your credit profile strong enough to qualify for a loan amount of $12,000? Do you even have a plan for paying for your education? If there is no plan, you plan to fail!

The first step in applying for financial aid is completing the Free Application for Federal Student Aid (FAFSA). The FAFSA allows the Department of Education to determine how much of the $150 billion in grants, work-study, and loans funds you are eligible to receive to help pay for educational expenses such as tuition, room & board, books, and other related fees. Educational institutions, government, and private agencies that provide educational funds use the information from the FAFSA as part of their determination to award the funds. Some colleges have their own financial aid application that a student must complete in addition to the FAFSA. Check the websites or call the Financial Aid Office at each school you are applying to. The reason for doing so is because there is limited space on the FAFSA to explain extenuating family circumstances. However, most institutional applications provide the student with the space to explain their unique circumstances.

The documents needed to complete the FAFSA are as follows (https://fafsa.ed.gov/):

- Computer with internet access (home, school, or library)
- Citizens—social security numbers (dependency status)
- Eligible noncitizens—alien registration card

- License number(s)
- W-2 or end of the year paystub
- Current tax returns—1040, 1040A, 1040EZ

    o **Important Note**: If current tax returns are not available, use prior year tax returns to help you complete the section on taxable, untaxable income, assets, and/or investments.

- End of the year Statements on checking and savings balances; real estate investment property, stocks, and bonds; and business income and investments
- School codes
- A cup of coffee, tea, juice, or water to calm your nerves!

Below are a few FAFSA questions to help you become familiar with the FAFSA form.

- **Personal Identification Number (PIN)**/www.pin. ed.gov—Used to access your personal information and as the student's digital signature
- **Student Demographics**—Student's name, SS#, DOB, address, marital status, gender, email, license#, citizenship, school status, parental education, high school
- **School Selection**—Includes the names of colleges of interest and their Federal school codes, if available

> **Note:** The FAFSA will supply you with the school code when you type the name of the school in the appropriate field provided.

- **Dependency Status**—A test to determine whether the student is dependent or independent
- **Parent Demographics**—The same info above if declared dependent status
- **Financial Information**—Includes financial income information, work-study, and/or grant/scholarship support; untaxed income-tax deferred pension; and child support received; checking/savings, real estate investment value, and business net worth
- **Sign and Submit**—Review information, digital signature with/ PIN, and submit
- **Confirmation**—Student Aid Report (SAR)

Once you are admitted to a college or university, that school will use the information you provided on the FAFSA to determine your financial award and will send your award letter to you. The award letter will let you know the total cost of attendance and will include a listing of available funding source; this is what is called financial aid.

A typical cost of attendance (COA) budget can look like this:

Budget or Cost of Attendance (COA)	Tuition, Room & Board, Books and Supplies, Transportation, and other fees
Expected Family Contribution (EFC)	Student or Family contribution toward tuition or cost of attendance

Need Formula: COA less (-) EFC = NEED
COA $25,000
EFC - $1,500
Need $23,500

There are several types of funding categories available to help students pay the cost of education.

Typical Undergraduate Financial aid package:	Fall Semester	Spring Semester
Pell Grant: $5,650	$2,825	$2,825
Hope Scholarship*: $5,000	$2,500	$2,500
Work-study: $2,000	$1,000	$1,000
Federal Loans: $10,850	$5,425	$5,425
Total: $23,500	$11,750	$11,750

*The Hope Scholarship is awarded to students who are residents in Georgia and meet the state's scholarship requirement.

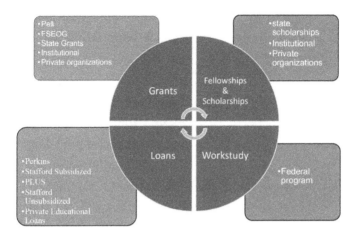

Paying for college will require a financial commitment. The primary responsibility rests with the student and his or her family for undergraduate education and the student alone for graduate school. Below are six (6) funding sources available to help students pay the cost of education.

Scholarships—These are financial awards that help students pay for college and do not have to be repaid. Funds are administered and awarded by several entities such as the government, colleges and universities, and private organizations. Scholarships can be awarded based on need and merit, need only, or merit only. Educational institutions call these restricted scholarships. Colleges and universities have two types of scholarship categories—Restricted and Unrestricted.

- University Restricted Scholarships/Grants: These are scholarships are awarded to students who meet certain requirements/restrictions (e.g., GPA, certain discipline, athletic field). Students should complete the necessary financial aid forms and applications to be considered for as much financial aid that is available.

Generally, scholarships do not have to be repaid, except if a student violates the scholarship requirements, withdraws from the program, or fails to meet enrollment guidelines.

- University Unrestricted Scholarships/Grants: Scholarships or grants awarded based on need and merit or need only. These awards have very few, if any, restrictions or requirements. The merit component in some cases is simply based on the strength of the student's admission application, thus, not requiring students to meet further obligations as an enrolled student.

Awards can range from $100.00 to full tuition awarded as a one-time single term award or awarded annually. There is a way to fund your college education. Thousands of scholarship opportunities are available. However, research is required to find 'free' money, and you must invest real time to locate the specific scholarships that meet your profile and complete each scholarship application.

Fellowships—These are financial awards that do not have to be repaid. Fellowships can be prestigious, merit-based only awards or merit and need-based. In certain instances, some fellowships can carry a stipend (additional free money often used for books, room & board, and/or supplies like computers). Some fellowships can be linked to specific research—certain faculty members may have available fellowships for graduate students and doctorial students to perform certain research in a discipline, or for a certain department or center. Fellowship funds are awarded by educational institutions or private organizations. Partial awards cover half of the school's tuition and full awards cover the entire tuition. One thing to keep in mind, however, is that a single fellowship that exceeds tuition and fees is considered taxable income. Some merit-based fellowships can carry a stipend. There are specific prestigious national and international fellowship opportunities that a student can add to their college or graduate experience (Fulbright or White House Fellowships); These awards often require essays and panel interviews.

Stipends—These are financial awards that accompany certain fellowships and can be considered taxable income.

Grants—These are financial awards that do not have to be repaid. Generally, grants are based on need: some institutional grants are awarded based on need and merit or need only. Grants are awarded and administered by several entities-the government, colleges and universities, and private organizations. The federal and state governments have many grant programs available to students. Pell-grants and FSEOG are federal programs awarded through the institutions by completing the FAFSA. These two programs are awarded to students from low income families. For a list of state specific grants, see your guidance counselor or go to this link:

http://www.collegescholarships.org/grants/state.htm,
Like scholarships, colleges and universities have two types of grant categories—Restricted and Unrestricted. The same criteria above apply.

- University Restricted Scholarships/Grants: Scholarships are awarded to students who meet certain requirements/restrictions (e.g., GPA, certain discipline, athletic field, etc.).
- University Unrestricted Scholarships/Grants: Scholarships or grants awarded based on need and merit or need only. These awards have very few, if any, restrictions or requirements.

Generally, grants are free funds that do not need to be repaid. In very rare instances, grants may have to be repaid. If a student's financial aid is disbursed to him or her and they withdraw from the program early in the semester, the student may be required to repay a portion or the total grant disbursed in that semester or trimester.

Research is essential to find hundreds of scholarships that fit your specific profile. Appendix C has a list of scholarship links with thousands of great scholarships, grants, and other forms of financial support.

> **Work Study**—These are student employment opportunities offset by the government and the college or university. The government provides students with the chance to gain work experience on campus to defray college costs and expenses. Like most jobs, students receive a paycheck and are expected to use the funds for educational purposes.
>
> **Loans**—These are borrowed funds that students use to pay for college costs that must be repaid.

Student loans, like any other loan, MUST Be REPAID. The Federal Loan Program includes Stafford Subsidized and Unsubsidized and the Perkins loan. The government pays the interest on subsidized loans while a student is in school, while the unsubsidized is accruing interest. The Perkins Loan has a low fixed interest and is awarded to students with high need, as defined by the FAFSA. These loans are administered by colleges and universities. Students must complete the FAFSA first before being awarded federal and private educational loans. Students should maintain satisfactory academic progress while receiving federal loans. If, however, a student's academic progress is compromised, he or she will be given a warning of probation. If academic trouble persists, then the student will not be awarded federal loans to cover tuition expenses. In order to restore federal loan eligibility, the student should see a financial aid counselor.

Once a student completes their program or withdraws from their program, the six-month grace period begins. The Department of Education has strict repayment terms and conditions, yet flexible repayment plans when repaying federal loans. These loans do not go away, except if participating in a forgiveness program or in the death of the borrower. Listen up! Even if you file bankruptcy, you still are obligated to repay your federal loans. While I am covering loan programs, I would be remised if I did not share important loan terms and discuss important repayment structures. Federal loans can be forgiven on certain terms when you participate in certain loan forgiveness programs.

Loan Forgiveness or Repayment

The federal government and some universities offer Loan Forgiveness Programs or Loan Repayment Programs. With loan forgiveness, if approved, a certain amount of the borrower's loan or, perhaps the total loan is forgiven, waived, or wiped clean, given the borrower has met the federal program's conditions or the university's program requirements. The Loan Repayment Assistance Program is different from the Loan Forgiveness Program. With a Loan Repayment Program, select universities offer to help students meet their monthly loan payments for a specified period if the borrower meets the eligibility requirements. A separate application is required and must be approved by the university. Borrowers should continue to pay their loans until they receive approval from the institution. They will also send the borrower documentation with exact dates.

Loan Deferment and Forbearance

Loan Deferment—This is a Federal Assistance Program that grants a student the option to reduce or temporarily stop their student loan monthly payments for a specified period.

Important Note: The Department of Education Appropriation Act of 2019 grants deferments for cancer patients currently in/on treatment.

Forbearance—This is a Federal Assistance Program for students facing economic hardship. Forbearance temporarily cease or stop a borrower's monthly payments or reduce payments for a specified time period.

Be Aware!!! With loan deferment and forbearance, consider the following:

- Interest is accruing on your federal loans.
- Borrowers have the option to pay the interest while in forbearance or let the interest accrue.
- If a student decides to let the interest accrue, it will be capitalized (added) to the principle of the loan, thus increasing the loan total or balance.

EXAMPLE: Total federal loan borrowing $37,500 repaid with the Standard Repayment Plan (10 Years/120 Months) at 7% interest. Monthly payments will be approximately $435 (Principle of $216 and Interest of $218). You can elect to pay the $218 while in forbearance or let it accrue.

If granted a 6 months forbearance, you will accrue $1,308 in interest.

Principle	$37,500	Principle	$37,500
Interest accruing	$0	Interest accruing	$218
Principle after Forbearance	$37,500	Principle after Forbearance	$38,808

Loan Repayment Plans

- **Standard Repayment Plan**—Repayment of loan is over 10-years with no prepayment penalties
- **Extended Repayment Plan**—Repayment of loan is extended over 25 years or 300 months

The loan payments start low and remain steady over 25 years. The danger of this plan is that you will repay approximately twice as much, if not three times as much, the amount you initially borrowed. In the end this student loan ($26,000 average loan debt) can look like an expensive mortgage. My advice to you is to make sure you explore all repayment plans before selecting this option. If this is the best plan that meets your situation, make as many prepayments as possible.

Graduated Repayment Plan—Repayment of loan over a 10-year period, starting with low monthly payments that gradually increase every two years. Although the payments start low in the beginning, the latter half of the loan balance with this repayment plan will be costly. This loan **MUST** be fully paid within 10 years. What you did not pay in the beginning, you will pay at the end.

Income-driven Repayment Plans (4 Plans)— Monthly payments are based on income and family structure (size and marital status). The repayment of the loan under this plan is extended to 12 yrs., 15 yrs., 18 yrs., or longer. Each year, you must renew your status (confirm income and family size). If you do not renew by a certain date established by the loan servicer, it may have an adverse effect on your credit.

Let me give you an idea how the different repayment plans compare and the total balance a student will pay between 10 and 30 years. The balance below represents the average total federal student loan at a 4-year public college. (Department of Education, studentloans.gov)

Average Loan Balance:	$26,946
Interest Rate:	3.9%
Family Size:	1 (Self with no dependents)
Marital Status:	Single
Adjusted Gross Income (AGI):	$37,000
State:	Georgia

Reference: https://studentloans.gov/myDirectLoan/repaymentEstimator.action

Student Loan Repayment Estimator

Standard Repayment Plan:

Student Borrower will pay a total
of **$32,585** over **120 months**
$272–$272/month

Graduated Repayment Plan:

You will pay a total of **$33,979** over **120 months**
$152–$455/month

Income-Based Repayment (IBR)

You will pay a total of **$34,553** over **146 months**
$166–$272/month

IBR for New Borrowers

You will pay a total of **$38,160** over **192 months**
$111–$272/month

Income Based --Revised Pay As You Earn (REPAYE)

You will pay a total of **$38,106** over **188 months**
$111–$332/month

Income Based--Pay As You Earn (PAYE)

You will pay a total of **$38,160** over **192 months**
$111–$272/month

Income-Contingent Repayment (ICR)

You will pay a total of **$36,444** over **189 months**

$174–$211/month

As you can see, each plan has a different monthly payment amount, total payments, and length of time committed (repayment duration) to repay the loan. The total amount of repayment can change when you add out-of-school Deferment or Forbearance to the mix, so be wise when it comes to selecting a repayment plan, because the interest can add up.

Default

You want to avoid going into default on your student loans at any cost. Default status can significantly affect your credit rating, employment opportunities, and impede your ability to apply for federal loans in the future, should you decide to return to college for an advance degree.

Consolidation

Consolidation is the act of combining all your federal debt with one servicer. For students who have federal loans with different lenders but want the ease of making one payment to one source, consolidation provides the pathway. This will require research on your part. Make sure you consider the interest rate and repayment terms when deciding to consolidate your student loan debt.

Tip 1   Create a financial plan.

Tip 2   Do your research and learn the types of
           financial aid that each school offers.

Tip 3   Research online or call the Financial Aid
           Office to inquire about the average grant
           amount offered to students. Get this infor-
           mation from every school you are interested
           in attending.

Tip 4   You should answer the following question:
           If the average grant does not cover tuition,
           are you in a position to borrow the balance?

Tip 5   (A MUST!) Commit to researching and
           applying for private and public scholarship/
           fellowship/grant opportunities. To increase
           your odds, it is recommended that you apply
           for more than 10 scholarships, especially
           bearing in mind, the cost of tuition.

Finally, you have reached the end of your first read. Now, READ it again! Go back and practice the principles and habits, ask yourself the probing questions, complete the journal exercises, rewrite your college essays, research scholarship opportunities, and create a strategic financial aid game plan. Then, after you have put in the necessary work, you will experience rewarding results.

Journal Exercise

What is the total cost to attend my top 5 schools of choice?

$ _____ $ _____

$ _____ $ _____

$ _____ $ _____

$ _____ $ _____

How much has my family saved toward my college education? $_____

Is my family savings enough to cover the costs above?

_____

Starting with the College Board, what are 20 scholarship opportunities you are eligible for?

_____

_____

_____

_____

_____

_____

_____

_____

_____

_____

_____

_____

_____

If you are already in college, how much have you
borrowed so far?

- Federal Loans (include the Perkins Loan)
  $_____

- Private Educational Loans
  $_____

APPENDIX A

PER the Bureau of Labor Statistics, here is a list of *Career Opportunities* and average (mean or median) salary: http://www.bls.gov/oes/current/naics2_11.htm

Profession	Average Wage	# Workers
ARCHITECTURE & ENGINEERING		
Architecture & Engineers	$ 96,000	57330
Architects, Landscape	$ 93,460	800
Engineers	$ 103,000	46600
Chemical Engineers	$ 126,000	900
Civil Engineers	$ 99,000	2550
Computer Engineers	$ 109,000	1290
Industrial Engineers	$ 92,450	12730
Mechanical Engineers	$ 89,370	7100
ARTS, DESIGN, ENTERTAINMENT, SPORTS & MEDIA		
Art Directors	$ 115,000	1890
Multimedia Artists & Animation	$ 65,270	450
Designers	$ 57,890	19510
Entertainers & Performers	$ 77,030	760
Actors & Producers	$ 87,360	560
Production Directors	$ 87,410	550
Dancers & Choreographers	$ 49,220	
Writers & Editors	$ 67,550	4920
BUSINESS & FINANCIAL OPERATIONS		
Buyers & Purchasing Agents	$ 66,170	1320
Claims Adjuster, Appraisers, Examiners, Investigators	$ 62,600	7630
Human Resources	$ 67,840	39850
Management Analysts	$ 90,160	42230
Financial Specialists	$ 79,920	195900
Budget Analysts	$ 79,940	3840
Financial Analysts	$ 88,700	49450

Credit Counselors, Loan Officers	$ 77,830	18820
Tax Examiners	$ 67,720	100
BUILDING & GROUNDS OCCUPATION		
First-line Supervisors, Landscaping, Lawn Services, Ground Keeping	$ 54,230	380
Building Cleaning	$ 26,030	8030
Grounds Maintenance	$ 29,720	1670
COMMUNITY & SOCIAL SERVICES		
Counselors	$ 44,010	5380
Education Counselors	$ 48,360	770
Social Workers	$ 48,950	8690
Religious Workers	$ 52,870	450
COMPUTER & MATHEMATICAL		
Computer & Information Researchers	$ 136,990	280
Computer Information Analysts	$ 89,610	59930
Software Developers	$ 95,560	72980
Computer Programmers	$ 82,630	13880
Computer Support Specialists	$ 56,840	42850
Mathematical Science	$ 89,400	12870
CONSTRUCTION & EXTRACTION		
Construction Trades & Extraction Workers	$ 74,340	2360
Carpenters	$ 45,360	740
Cement, Masons	$ 52,690	90
Construction Operators	$ 37,690	1680
Plumbers, Steamfitters	$ 67,240	480
Oil, Gas, Mining Workers	$ 63,880	210
EDUCATION		
Vocational Teacher	$ 41,000	30
Preschool, Primary & Secondary & Special Education Teachers	$ 33,990	880
Adult Education & Literacy	$ 46,950	120
Librarians	$ 62,870	410
Substitute Teachers	$ 33,240	230
FARMING, FISHING, FORESTRY		
Fishing & Forestry	$ 36,010	490
Agricultural Workers	$ 27,060	
First-line Supervisors	$ 61,760	120

FOOD PREPARATION OCCUPATION		
Food Preparation Services	$ 32,760	13620
Chef & Head Cooks	$ 59,100	980
First-line Supervisors	$ 44,110	6080
Cooks & Food Preparation Workers	$ 25,760	2540
Food & Beverage	$ 22,630	3980
Bartenders	$ 31,090	220
Waiters/Waitresses	$ 22,670	1460
Cooks (Fast food)	$ 21,970	
HEALTH TECHNOLOGISTS		
Clinical Lab Tech	$ 58,730	420
Health technologists	$ 47,050	10860
Diagnostic Techs	$ 73,550	550
Cardio Techs	$ 55,170	40
Health Practitioners	$ 37,050	1130
Surgical Techs	$ 44,980	
Occupational Health	$ 76,020	2920
Athletic Trainers	$ 50,450	60
HEALTHCARE PRACTIONERS		
Healthcare Practitioners	$ 73,590	33200
Health Diagnosis & Test Practitioners	$ 89,520	18480
Dentists	$ 165,340	
Pharmacists	$ 119,650	2590
Physicians & Surgeons	$ 221,940	790
Psychiatrists	$ 199,410	80
Therapists	$ 75,320	1520
Occupational Therapist	$ 79,080	280
Respiratory Therapist	$ 54,740	60
Speech Pathologist	$ 85,660	270
Veterinarians	$ 130,430	80
Nurse Practitioners	$ 99,160	390
Registered Nurse	$ 76,220	11770

Profession	Average Wage	# Workers
HEALTHCARE SUPPORT		
Healthcare Support Workers	$ 35,310	6670
Nursing, psychiatric & Home Aides	$ 27,630	1880
Occupational Therapy Assistants	$ 58,870	180
Physical Therapist Assistant	$ 55,270	440
Medical Assistant	$ 32,870	1560
Pharmacy Aides	$ 38,060	60
Phlebotomists	$ 31,080	280
INSTALLATION, MAINTENANCE & REPAIR		
Installation & Maintenance Repair	$ 50,760	41560
First-line Supervisors	$ 72,030	5480
Electrical & Electronic Equipment Workers	$ 52,850	4500
Radio & Telecommunications	$ 59,280	1650
Misc. Electrical Equipment	$ 59,360	1510
Vehicle & Mobile Equipment	$ 49,170	3920
Auto Tech	$ 45,150	710
Tire Repair Worker	$ 30,810	
Control Valve	$ 64,990	590
Industrial Machinery	$ 53,920	1950
Line Installers	$ 66,170	1920
Precision Instrument & Equipment Repair	$ 55,860	1020
Misc. Installation	$ 40,410	1970
Maintenance Repair	$ 43,050	18690
LEGAL OCCUPATION		
Lawyers & Judges	$ 175,710	17110
Legal occupations	$ 139,580	25400
Arbitrators & Mediators	$ 87,760	40
Legal Support	$ 65,060	8290
LIFE, PHYSICAL & SOCIAL SCIENCE		
Physical & Social Scientists	$ 96,370	16880
Life Scientists	$ 96,990	6090
Agricultural & Food Scientists	$ 89,740	2640
Biological Scientists	$ 102,980	
Conservation Scientists	$ 67,340	210
Medical Scientists	$ 106,720	1590
Physical Scientists	$ 119,710	6070

Chemists & Material Scientists	$ 86,080	2520
Environmental Scientists	$ 140,990	2790
Social Scientists	$ 89,330	770
Economists	$ 107,930	240
Psychologists	$ 82,420	410
Agricultural Technician	$ 32,000	
Anthropologists/ Archeologists	$ 50,000	
MANAGEMENT		
Top Executives	$ 165,920	108950
Senior Managers	$ 142,620	447960
Chief Executives	$ 220,700	20620
Advertising, Marketing, Public Relations, & Sales Managers	$ 144,080	73250
Operations Managers	$ 139,260	178260
Administrative Managers	$ 109,260	17610
Financial Managers	$ 154,640	68460
Human Resource Managers	$ 133,360	19230
Education Administration Managers	$ 72,500	1310
Property & Real Estate Managers	$ 101,610	6220
Other Managers	$ 129,560	37570
PERSONAL CARE SERVICE		
Supervisors	$ 41,360	100
Animal Trainers	$ 30,230	4640
PRODUCTION OCCUPATION		
First-line Supervisors	$ 68,120	4610
Production Occupation	$ 46,580	24570
Electrical & Electronic Workers	$ 38,040	
Bakers	$ 74,550	
Butchers & Meat Cutters	$ 34,870	90
Food Processor Workers	$ 25,620	
Tailors & Dressers	$ 32,220	100
Jewelers	$ 51,070	190
Painters	$ 36,610	190
PROTECTIVE SERVICES OCCUPATION		
Protective Services	$ 26,220	440
Security Guards	$ 26,300	430
Correctional Officer/Jailer	$ 36,000	
Firefighter	$ 55,000	

Transit/Railroad Police	$ 47,000	
SALES		
Sales Workers	$ 62,190	1790
Sales Representative	$ 61,970	420
First-line Supervisors	$ 75,900	80
Cashiers	$ 25,370	
Retail Sales Worker	$ 26,700	
TRANSPORTATION		
Transportation Operator	$ 32,150	40910
Supervisors	$ 45,780	1370
Aircraft Pilots	$ 89,330	1660
Motor Vehicle Operators	$ 37,330	13550
Drivers	$ 37,340	13540
Other Transportation	$ 32,200	

APPENDIX B

STEAM/STEM Information

- Department of Education (ed.gov/STEM)
- STEM Educational Coalition (stemedcoalition.org)
- College Board Advance AP (apcentral.collegeboard. org) (pre-app.collegeboard.org/start-and-grow)
- 100 Black Men (100blackmen-atlanta. org/100-robotics/)

U.S. News and World Report, Best STEM high Schools (Reviewed and ranked the best high school's in math and science educational STEM fields).

These are the top 10:

Ranked #1--High Technology High School, Lincroft, New Jersey (national ranking #11)

Ranked #2—Early College of Guilford, Greensboro, North Carolina (national ranking #23)

Ranked #3—Thomas Jefferson High School in Science and Technology, Alexandria, Virginia (national ranking #5)

Ranked #4—Basis Scottsdale, Scottsdale, Arizona
(national ranking #2)

Ranked #5--Whitney High School, Cerritos, California
(national ranking #19)

Ranked #6—Basis Tucson North, Tucson, Arizona
(national ranking #3)

Ranked #7--Raleigh Charter High School, Raleigh,
North Carolina (national ranking #37)

Ranked #8—International Community School,
Washington (national ranking #178)

Ranked #9—Academy of Allied Health and Science,
Neptune, New Jersey (national ranking #189)

Ranked #10—Troy High School, Fullerton, California
(national ranking #432)

*For additional high school rankings go to http://
www.usnews.com/education/best-high-schools/
national-rankings/stem.

Online College Resources:

National Association for College Admission Counseling
(nacacnet.org)

Connections Academy (connectionsacademy.com)

Khan Academy (khanacademy.org)

Udemy (udemy.com)

Coursera (coursera.org)

edX (edx.org)

Harvard (online-learning.harvard.edu/catalog/free)

Yale (poorvucenter.yale.edu/online-courses)

APPENDIX C

To make your grant search easier, here is a short list of scholarships and links with hundreds of financial aid opportunities:

The College Board Scholarship Opportunity	Asian & Pacific Islander American Scholarship Fund	AXA Achievement Scholarship
JP Morgan- Thomas G. Labrecque Smart Start Program	Jack Kent Cooke Foundation College Scholarship	Microsoft Tuition Scholarship
USDA National Scholars Program	Regeneron Science Talent Search (STEM)	Dr. Pepper Tuition Giveaway
ROTC Army	Flinn Foundation Scholarships	Dell Scholars Program
Coca-Cola Scholars Program	Gensler Diversity Scholarship	Horatio Alger National Scholarship (need-based)
National Honor Society Scholarship	UNCF Stem Scholars Program	Walmart Associate Scholarship
National Black MBA Association (NBMBAA)	Ron Brown Scholars Program	Herbert Lehman Educational Foundation Scholarships
The Reverend Pinckney Scholarships	The Jackie Robinson Foundation	The Gates Scholarship Program
Army Women's Foundation Legacy Scholarship	Berklee Lollapalooza Endowed Scholarships	First Responders Children's Foundation General Scholarships
George M. Pullman Education Foundation Scholarship	Hispanic School Fund College Scholarship	Harry S. Truman Scholarship Foundation

Woodrow Wilson National Fellowship Program	Ronald Reagan Presidential Foundation & Institute	Discovery Education
Foot Locker Foundation	Public Policy and International Affairs Program	

This is, in no way, a comprehensive list of scholarship, fellowship, and grant opportunities available. There are thousands of alternatives. For a more thorough scholarship search, please see the links below. The aim of Ivy Style Preparation (ISP) Series I is to provide the Financial Aid fundamentals. ISP Series II will cover Financial Aid specifics and college funding opportunities.

Scholarship Search Sites:

- http://www.finaid.org/
- http://www.gmsp.org/
- https://studentaid.ed.gov/sa/
- https://bigfuture.collegeboard.org/
- http://www.fastweb.com/
- http://www.collegescholarships.com/
- https://www.newusafunding.com/
- http://scholarshipzone.com/
- https://scholarships.uncf.org/
- http://brownvboard.org/
- http://foundation.walmart.com/
- http://thurgoodmarshallfund.net/
- http://www.nsbe.org/Programs/Scholarships
- http://www.akaeaf.org/

- http://www.nabainc.org/

The above 2017 programs are not intended to be an exhaustive search of financial aid resources. Let this list serve as a start to your search for financial assistance.

ENDNOTES AND REFERENCES

Where Do I Start?

1. Covey, Stephen. *The 7 Habits of Highly Successful People*. Illinois: Free Press (Simon and Schuster), 1989.
2. Covey, Sean. *7 Habits of Highly Successful Teens*. Illinois:Touchstone Books (Simon & Schuster), 1998.
3. Leaf, Caroline. *Who Switched Off My Brain? Controlling toxic thoughts and emotions*. USA: Improv, Ltd, 2009. Dirty Dozen

Is College for me?

4. Investopedia, New York: www.Investopedia.com.
5. U.S. Department of Education, National Center for Education Statistics. *Digest of Education Statistics, 2017* (NCES 2018-070), 2019.
6. Association of American Colleges & Universities (AACU, Spring 2013) (Pryor et al. 2011, 9; emphasis mine)

What should I Consider When Selecting Schools?

7. U.S. Department of Education, Science, Technology, Engineering, and Math, including Computer Science (STEM). Department: STEM Lead and Policy Advisor, Office of Planning, Evaluation, and Policy Development — Jean Morrow. https://www.ed.gov/stem

8. U.S. News and World Report, *Why Does Diversity Matter at College Anyway?* Jeremy S. Hyman and Lynn F. Jacobs. (August 2009). https://www.usnews.com/education/blogs/professors-guide/2009/08/12/why-does-diversity-matter-at-college-anyway.

What Do I look like on paper?

9. College Board, New York: https://www.collegeboard.org/.

10. Fastweb, Massachusetts: https://www.fastweb.com/ and

11. Fastweb, Massachusetts: https://www.fastweb.com/college-search/articles/summer-programs-for-high-school-students (Summer Extracurricular Programs)

12. Peter Thiel, Thiel Fellowship. Montana: https://thielfellowship.org/.

13. Forbes. *The World's Billionaires* (3/6/2018) https://www.forbes.com/billionaires/list/;9/#version:static.

How do I start the Essays?

14. Alex Kendrick, *Facing the Giants*, 2006.
http://www.kendrickbrotherscatalogue.com/facingthegiants/.

15. Rutgers University, New Jersey: https://www.rutgers.edu/.

How Am I going to Pay?

16. U.S. Department of Education, Free Application for Federal Student Aid (FAFSA).
Department: Office of Federal Student Aid, https://studentaid.gov/h/apply-for-aid/fafsa.

17. U.S. Department of Education, Student Loans Repayment. Department: Office of Federal Student Aid, https://studentaid.gov/app/repaymentEstimator.action.

FROM THE DESK
OF THE AUTHOR

"Ask not what your country can do for you, but what you can do for your country." ~ *Former Headmaster for the late President John F. Kennedy, Jr.*

THIS was my mission for more than 15 years, and these words still shape and influence my life today. During my tenure at Harvard University Kennedy School of Government (HKS) in Cambridge, Massachusetts, I served in many roles, including former Director of Student Financial Services (Financial Aid). While assuming a full workload, I pursued a master's degree; at Harvard University.

My experience at Harvard has afforded me extraordinary opportunities to cross paths with some amazing leaders. Whether a gentle smile, an encouraging word, or a pat on the back, these individuals made my tenure at Harvard much more memorable. Yet, it was the Institute of Politic's (IOP) forum events where my experience as a manager and future business owner was sealed. In my opinion, the IOP was the icing on the cake. Besides Hollywood and New York, where else could you go to meet such world changers like the honorable Ellen Johnson Sirleaf, former President George W. Bush, Barbara Streisand, Oliver Stone, the late Johnny Cochran, John Kennedy, Jr., Teddy Kennedy, and many more global leaders? It is without question that I learned the most from the relationship between administrator and students, for the students demonstrated such strength, perseverance, determination, and tenacity. I consider it an honor to have served at the Kennedy School in my varying capacities!

I humbly share my story with you, my reader, to let you know that I come with a wealth of knowledge, experience, and insight to impart. As an educational consultant for more than 10 years, I have been asked many questions at one-on-one sessions, group meetings, and even through social media forums about course curriculums, college tours, admissions applications, essays, and the overwhelming financial aid process. Thus, it prompted me to write this book to answer some commonly asked questions about the process and share tips, tools, and secrets you can use to submit a more robust application.

SPECIAL ACKNOWLEDGMENTS

D'edra Armstrong, you are a person of many words. Your gift of words touches the inner recesses of the soul (a.k.a, *The Soul's Solace*). Although your schedule was full, drafting three books, you found time to offer your editorial services. Thank you! I cannot wait for the release of your masterpieces. You are the world's best kept secret. But wait until 2020!

Dr. Brenda Dickerson, you have always had a desire to see students change their lives and transform their communities. You taught me so much about leadership and standing by what I believe. Thank you for your insight and rendering your editorial services.

Dr. Cecil & Brenda Hale, I always heard that God puts people in your life for a season or a lifetime. Who would have thought I would be connected to you both for more than 23 years? Thank you for reviewing the book and offering your feedback. I look forward to touring the country with you both.

Maritza Hernandez, you are a first-class Associate Dean. Thank you for carving time out of your busy schedule of overseeing Enrollment Services at the Harvard School of Education and taking care of your family. While preparing for Thanksgiving, you

did me a favor and reviewed the book. Thank you!
You are a beautiful person and a wonderful friend.

Michelle Thornhill & Wayne Thornhill, Esq., the
epitome of Excellence. You have been such an
inspiration in my life. Your heart to mentor and
empower everyone around you, particularly young
men, is commendable. I am simply amazed how
God brought our families together. Thank you,
Michelle, for taking time out of your extremely busy
schedule to review the manuscript and forward your
feedback. I love you dearly and look forward to
seeing you continue to live your best life.

Dr. Constance Shabazz, you walked with me through
this tedious journey. How can I thank you enough,
especially when I placed the manuscript on the
shelf after feeling overwhelmed with research and
writing? I truly appreciate your insight and wisdom
as the Literary Queen. Thank you for the one-
on-one's when you traveled to Atlanta or the long
phone calls, as you prepared to leave the country for
a couple of weeks. You are a godsend, and I love
you for challenging and stretching me.

Special Thanks: Murray Family, Ellzey Family, Delashment Family, Rising Phenomenal Women International, Inc., Rod Mullice, Maya Dillard Smith, Chip Joyner, Teia Beggs, Bryan Hancock, Gregg Harris, Alexandra Martinez, and Prella Hollie

CPSIA information can be obtained
at www.ICGtesting.com
Printed in the USA
BVHW080517240920
589460BV00004B/425

9 780578 640488